# Blood On My Typewriter
R.J. Avenira

"There is nothing to writing.
All you do is sit down at a
typewriter and bleed."

-Ernest Hemmingway

# CHAPTER ONE:

# DEMONS AND DEVILS

## Smoking at Night

There's nothing I love quite as
much
as smoking out the window
In the dead of night

Maybe it's the flicker
Of the lighter
Or the way the smoke
drifts up to the stars
Like a cloud

Maybe it's the ember
of the end of the cigarette
Coming to life
as I inhale

The life of the thing, though
Is the incredible feeling
Of peace
Gently flowing
Out of my lungs

Truly, truly, nothing compares
To smoking out the window
In the dead of night

## While You Still Can

Don't fall in love with me
Get away
Get away, sweet woman
While you still can

## Learning To Fly

I tried to escape
These bounds of hate

I tried to fly
Never saying goodbye

I tried it all
And still I fall

Back to the ground
Without a sound

## The Virtue of Day-Drinking

You know it's bad
When you start making excuses
For drinking
In the morning

But they don't understand
The need to escape
Into a bottle
Of whiskey or wine

Don't lecture me
I know what I'm doing
I know I'm hurting myself
I don't care
It hurts less
Than thinking about everything
I've done

## Before It Kills Us

It always seems like a good idea
Picking up girls
At a bar

They're the same type
Of lost, wayward soul
That I am

And I think I see
Too much of myself
In their glassy eyes

As we smoke a blunt
Out the window
Before fucking again

Let's do it again
Let's kill the pain
Before it kills us

## Escape While You Can

Beware
Pretty, sad, brown eyes
That whisper of darkness
While sucking the soul
Out of you

Beware
Beautiful women
With dark pasts

For they
Will ruin your life

And if you don't
Get out
Fast enough

You might just
Want them to

## The Woman

Sometimes I still see her face
Awakening
From both nightmares and day-
dreams

I can't tell whether I will ever
hate her
For what she did
More than I'll love her
For who she was

# In Love With Harmful Memories

I still think about it
sometimes.

The way it felt
So much better
Than anything else in the world

It's a craving
That will never go away

And I can't help
But love the memory

And honestly
Every day I yearn
To go back
To self-destruction

That's what it feels like
To get addicted
Off of just one hit

What if I hadn't stopped
In time?

Never start
If you have that choice.

## Sinner

If I stumbled
drunkenly
Into that church
and declared my sins
begging for forgiveness

Would they even hear me
rather than judge me
by my raggedy clothes
and ripped jeans
with cigarette burns
like bullet holes
making me a dead man

No, fuck them
and fuck that building

If there's a god
They couldn't keep him prisoner
In that box
Of greed and judgement

## On Romanticization

I'm sorry if it seems
That I'm romanticizing bad
things

That is human nature
And though I'd never wish
These experiences
On anyone else

I need to confess
What I have done

So please
Do not follow in my footsteps
But let me tell you
Where I have been

## My Father's Son

I remember the way
My dad slammed the front door
In my face
As I stumbled home by foot
After a long day
Of day-drinking, car sex,
and running from the cops

He wanted a son
Who would live up
To his expectations-
I'm sorry I never could.

I'm sorry, father
For I was born to be a wanderer
And though we share blood
It seems our DNA couldn't be
More different

I know I should hate you
For how you treated me
But I only feel sorry for you
That I could never live up
To what you wanted.

## The Reader Pt. I

In some ways
I hate you
For reading this

For absorbing my pain
and living through it
With all of the thrill
And none of the consequence

In some ways
I resent
How you can think
You know me
Even though
You know
Only a shadow
Of who I am

## The Reader Pt. II

In some ways I love you
For allowing me
To share my pain

It unburdens me
To share this
With the world
And that is something
Therapy can't buy

## The All-Knowing Therapist

She takes her little notes
On that judgmental clip board
As I reply to her questions

Does she think
she understands
my pain?
Does she think
she understands
who I am?

Maybe she's already diagnosed me
Already thinks she knows me
Has already narrowed down
All of my 'problems'
And categorized me
Waiting to put me in line
Like a cow waiting
For the guillotine
To be turned into a product
For society to consume

I hate her, I do
I hate all of them
The way they think
They could fix me
When I don't want to be fixed
—At least, not by them.
I could never give them the
satisfaction.

## The Girl Who Disappeared

She was the antidote
To who I was

She was the only one
I would've let change me
Into someone better

She was everything
But she disappeared
One fall morning

She left town
Changed her number
And changed her name

And I will always wonder
What could've been
Had she stayed

## Different

I could never identify myself
With a group

People love to generalize
And categorize
Who you are

I'm not like them
You can't lump me in
With the rest of them
I'm different
And I won't let you
Think otherwise

## The Night of February 14

Valentines day
Is the best day
For hookups
With other broken souls.

We briefly entertain the idea
That perhaps
We could find love
In this bar
Tonight

I locked eyes with her
From across the room
And I knew..

Her lips
Tasted like Brandy
Her pussy
Tasted like Hennessy

Her words
Hit me like a rush from a needle
Her lust
Tasted like cheap vodka

She left
Before I woke up
In the morning
-Thank god.

## Coming To Terms With Tragedy

We were in love
And she killed herself

That's as bluntly
As I can say it
There's no way around the truth

The thing is,
We are not cures
For other peoples' problems

It took me a decade
To forgive myself
For not being
What I could've been
For her

All I can say
Is treasure her
While you have her
Because you might not get to
Forever

## Love Is The Flicker of a Lighter

Love is not a roaring flame
Spreading and consuming all else

Love is the flicker of a lighter
It lasts for but a moment

And to watch it
In the dead of night

Is beautiful

## The Punishment of Sisyphus

Sleep, oh sleep
Where art thou?

Why hast thou forsaken me?

Sleep is the god
Who gives and takes
As he pleases

The insomniac
Is the sinner
Who is punished
For all eternity

Rolling over and over
Trying to escape
The land of the living

## Exorcism of the Soul

How can you cast out your demons
When, in truth,
You'll always be in love
To some degree
With how they make you feel?

This is the impossibility
Of this task
The exorcism of the soul
Which we all must perform
Against our own wills.

# CHAPTER TWO:

# SOULLESS SIRENS

## The Soulless Siren

She called to me
Through the fog
As I steered my fishing boat
In the moonlight

The siren's song
Irresistible
Answering an echo
Deep within my bones

This is the story
Of how I lost my heart
To a soulless siren

## Fantasy

She pursed her lips
Crossed her legs
Took a sip of her wine glass

I had never been so interested

It was as if she was created
Straight from the depths
of my deepest fantasy

## Sex In The Air

Sultry tunes
Seeped out
Of that vinyl player

Jazz music
Sex in the air
I sat next to her
With a smile

## The Match Soon Aflame

"I've been many places,"
She said to me,
"but nowhere as terrifying
as up in the air
voyaging through the clouds
-Flying. It is the most
terrifying
and yet the most beautiful
and amazing
part of life."

A former addict, like me
Looking for thrills
To fill the empty spaces
Within

What a match, I thought

Little did I know
That this match would ignite
And burn down my life

## Vicarious

I could almost see it
In my mind's eye
As she went on and on

I could almost feel
The thrill
Coursing through my blood

I could almost feel
What she felt

The feeling of running away
Escaping the past
Through blunt force

If only I could be so brave..

## The First Kiss

I kissed her
And she kissed me back
So hard
I tasted blood

I wanted more

## A Force of Nature

She fucked me
Like a tornado
A Volcano
A force of nature

It was rough
And passionate
We were loud enough
To shake the walls

The orgasm she gave me
Was like being hit
by lightning

## More

We laid there, moonlight
filtering in through the window
Chests heaving, recovering
From something almost
supernatural

Some sort of raw power
Raw attraction
I regretted nothing
And knew that soon enough
We would both be craving
more

## The Dawn

I woke up the next morning
And noticed she had left
I got up, body aching
But mind at peace

There it was, on the bedside
table
A note, with her phone number
Scribbled on it

## Blindfolded

She had blindfolded me
And I was in the passenger seat
Of her car
She drove as fast as her car
could go
I was afraid for my life
But thrilled at the same time

We stopped suddenly
And she led me outside
And kissed me hard
Ripping off the blindfold

I looked out over the city
And the sky full of stars

I looked into her eyes
And she smiled back at me
With a hint of mania

What had I gotten myself into?

## Secrets Spilled Like Blood

Tell me your fears
Tell me your secrets
Spill them
Like blood
And lets get drunk
On each other's souls
Like perverse vampires

Let me taste
Who you are

Don't you dare
Hold anything back
From me

## I Touched Her

We talked about conspiracy
theories
We talked about aliens
We talked about lust
Love
And death

I swear I touched who she was
And understood her
Like I had never understood
Anyone else

## Do Us Part

I could see myself
Spending the rest
Of my life
With this woman

I awoke one morning
With that
Terrifying realization

## May 24th

She sat me down
At the edge of the bed
Solemn and scared

I asked what was wrong
And after a pause
She told me

And those two words
Scared me more
Than anything ever had
Before..

"I'm pregnant."

## The World Crumbled

Panicked and afraid, I stood and
backed away from her

She grimaced
And I felt the world
Crumble around me

## Escape Into The Bottle

I ran out of that house
Not knowing what to do
Was this the end
Of my life
As I knew it?

I could never be a good father.
I wasn't ready.

So I did what I always do
The only thing I know how to do
I escaped
Into a bottle
And another, and another
Until I was too drunk
To be scared.

## God is a Cruel Motherfucker

"How can we have a baby together
When I don't even know your
middle name? How could this
happen?"

"There is a god, and he is one
cruel motherfucker."

## Cruel Happiness

I woke up
to the sound of her screaming
It was a miscarriage

As I held her
And comforted her
I secretly breathed
A sigh of relief

I looked out the window
At the sky full of stars
And thanked them for this luck

I vowed to leave
While I had the strength

## Reflections of the Self

I'm such a piece of shit.

I know, you must be thinking it
As I tell you the truth
Of what I did

Don't judge me
You would've done
The same thing

## Vignettes of Revenge

The whole story flashed before
my eyes
Vignette after vignette

I snapped back to the present
Looking back at the letter
In my hand

An invitation
To her wedding
To a new man

How she found me
After all these years
I don't know

Why would she send it?
Spite? Hatred? Reconciliation?

The seed of a though began
To bloom within me
As I tried to push it down
"I wish I had stayed-
I wish that was me."

## Whisky and Telephones

With a careless hand
I pushed the whisky bottle
Off the table

It shattered
On that hardwood floor
Into a hundred shards

Looking down at it
I sighed
And picked up a large piece

I pressed it against my throat
And nearly slashed it across

But the phone rang
And saved my life

X

## CHAPTER THREE:

# THE VIOLENT MEETING OF WILLS

## Sleep and Wake

I never learn
From my mistakes
I never give
More than I take
I never heal
More than I break
And the lines are blurred
Of sleep and wake

## The Validity of Viewpoints

We are all just
regurgitating
What we were taught

Does anyone
Have a point of view
That is their own
At all?

## The Taste

I can't taste orange juice
anymore

Without thinking
Of all the times I've used it
To mask the taste
Of alcohol

At least, before I grew
To love it

## Customers of Death

We are all just
Customers
At the door of death
All waiting in line
Waiting
For what we
Want most

## Control

I took the whisky bottle
In my hand
And I crushed it
Into a thousand pieces

As the blood ran down
My arms
I smiled
At last, at last
Feeling some control
Over my miserable life

## Burn It All

I took all of my savings
Out of the bank
—Not sure why—
And stashed them
Under my bed

Drunk, later that night
I finally knew why
I had done it.

With a grin
I put the money
On the table
Lit a cigarette
Took a puff
(I could never waste one)
And dropped it on the pile

With a maniacal grin
I watched my material worth
—Society's value of me—
Go up in flames

I laughed
And drank deeply
Finally satisfied

<u>R. J.</u>

I was given my father's name
I never asked for it, of course
And I'm pretty sure
If he could take it back
He would

## All That Drinkin'

They're always telling me
To look out for my liver
All that drinking
Won't do ya no good

I know damn well
What I'm doing
I'm trying to kill myself
I've just been
Too much of a coward
To do it all at once.

## Mushroom Mushroom on the Wall

She offered me mushrooms
And I took them
Slipping them
Into a PB&J

As the world took on a new shape
I laughed and giggled
Giving in to the thrill
With all my heart

I looked into my own face
And was disappointed
That I did not look
Like a demon

I thought perhaps
This substance
Would at last illuminate me
For what I really am

I shrugged
And turned back
To my typewriter
Writing out the truth
Even if the mirror
Wouldn't show it

## Kill Bill I

The bills
Have been stacking up
On the kitchen counter
Faster than ever

I don't care

I took the closest envelope
And rolled a blunt
With the paper inside
Without even looking
At what it was

I sighed
As the first bit of smoke
Hit my lungs

## Everything is the Same

I love the way
The music pulses
The lyrics don't matter
Everything fades
Everything is the same

Everything
Is
The
Same

## Their Control Pt. I

"Money doesn't buy you
happiness"
Is the biggest fucking lie
The elites ever made
The masses believe

They just want
To keep it all
To themselves

All the wealth
All the money
Lining their pockets

## Their Control Pt. II

The idea of an afterlife
Is made up
And perpetuated
By criminal elites
Who want the masses
To remain sedated
Accepting their shit lives
Believing it'll all equal out
In some fantasy afterlife

It's all a lie
It's all a lie
It's all a lie

## Their Control Pt. III

The worst people in the world
Are the ones
Who would rather accept
A comfortable stasis
Rather than join the fight
For positive change

## Their Control Pt. IV

They present their opinions
So transparently
Through films and TV
Expecting the masses
To lap it up
And believe in ideologies
That are pushed on them
by the powerful

## Vengeance

Take your revenge
While you can
Even the score
Whatever it takes

Peace is a lie
Take your vengeance

## Dark.

Darkness
Is not the enemy
All of my most trying moments
Have found me in the dark
On the verge of passing out
Drunk
As the darkness comforts me

## The Answer

Remember
That death
Is not always
the enemy

It
Can be
The answer

# The Ugly Truth About Selfishness

To be perfectly honest, I find it ridiculous when people say things like "suicide is selfish". No, what's selfish is making someone continue on living in an existence they can't endure. It's selfish to demand that someone keep living when their brain chemistry denies them happiness without being fucked up on a dozen drugs at a time. As the scripture says, "do not give a serpent to someone who asks for bread." Bread is death and the serpent is a life of torture.

That's the honest truth of it all. That's how I feel. Call me cruel, call my cynical, but don't dare lecture to me. You don't fucking understand.

x

# CHAPTER FOUR:

PROVING THEM WRONG

## Proving Them Wrong

They said
I would be dead
by 22

They said
I would be on the streets
And dead

Well here I am
Proving them wrong

## The Good Life

I'm not one
For pithy sayings
Or accepting advice
On how to live
Your own life

But I hope that
Even if I can't life
A good life
Myself

Perhaps I can tell someone else
How it might be done

## Ordinary

I can't tell you
What to be
All I can tell you
Is that the worst
Fucking thing
You could be
Is ordinary

## I've Come To Tell My Truths

I know what they'll say about
me. They'll say I preach taking
drugs, alcoholism, suicide. But
they don't fucking understand.
They see my truths and my open,
bleeding heart as an
inconvenient exception to the
rules society has carefully laid
out. They don't want me to say
what I've come to say- they'll
call me profane and absurd. They
don't want me to defy their
precious order. But I will. Fuck
them all. I've come to tell my
truths, and I damn well will.

## A Butterfly In Chains

What an ugly thing it is
To see everything beautiful
Be pimped out for money

## You Will Be Made Whole

You might be suffering
You might be broken
You might feel as if you
Are on your deathbed

But take heart
You will rise above all that
You will fix yourself
It will take time
But you will be
Made whole

## Freedom

You are as free
As you let yourself be

You don't have to listen
When society tells you
What to do
Commanding you like a dog
What behaviors are acceptable

Be yourself
Anything else
Is pointless.

## Finding Is Losing

I've found myself
Drifting off into daydreams
More and more lately

I've lost myself
Waking up from them
More every day

## Shell

Black, white, asian, gay
Whatever you are
We are all drunken bodies
At the same party
Trying desperately
To find
who we are

Why the fuck
Does this outward shell
Matter?

## Find Your Way

She was a girl lost in finding
herself, in love with the idea
that she could be different,
that she could be the one to
actually do it, to actually make
a difference.

He was a man given to drinking
and smoking, appealing to broken
hearts with issues, let's not
sugarcoat anything.

They met one October morning as
the first leaves of fall began
to drift downwards to the
ground.

Whether they decide to use each
other or build each other up is
the question. The answer isn't
written here- the answer will be
lived out by you- for we all
find pieces of ourselves in
other people, and it's our job
to make the best of the puzzle
we are putting together that we
call life. Find your way.

## Do Not Give an Inch

Do not be timid.

Do not hide your opinions, do not hold back who you are. Roar like a lion and demand the respect you deserve. Do not give an inch of ground to anyone who would stand in your way.

I tell you this again, do not be timid. For the love of god, do not be timid.

x

# CHAPTER FIVE:

FUCK WHAT THEY THINK

## I will never be your pawn

Do not play me for a fool
I will remember every slight
I will not forget
What you do to me

## Fuck What They Think

Be what you want
That's all that matters

## If I Ever Turn My Life Around

I got a letter
From my sister
Today

She wanted to know
If I was doing okay
She always did worry about me

I told her I was okay, of course
If I ever turn my life around
It'll be for her

## Love X

Love is not something
Set in stone

Love is a whisper
In a breeze
Flittering
From place to place

Love is a monument
To minutes and milliseconds
Spent in a state
Incomparable to anything else
It's an all-encompassing label
For so many things

## Enchanting & Terrifying

I took one look
Into her eyes
And saw something
Simultaneously enchanting
And terrifying

The chaos of a woman
Unafraid of who she is
A force of nature
Powerful and beautiful

I took one look into her eyes
And knew what I wanted

A-25060

Do you act the way you do
Because that's who you are
Or because that's the way
Society
Has ordered you to act?

## Everything You Are

I don't think there's any use
In trying to hold back
Your inner evil

Why pretend you're all good?
All the most interesting people
Aren't saints

So be real
Be human
Be honest
About everything you are

## No Bottles To Hide Behind

The wine
Started tasting like water
Only the harder stuff
Does it for me now

Maybe I should cut back
But if I do
I'll have to come face to face
With the worst parts of me
No bottles to hide behind

And that
Is exactly
What I'm afraid of

## Infrastructure

I just want
To get away
From this hole
I've dug myself
Further and further into
With every passing day

## My First Drink

I remember
I was just 13
When I stole my first
Bottle of Jack
A hobo was passed out on the
street
Clinging to his bottle solace
Gingerly, I stepped over to him
And stole the bottle from him.
It was half empty already, but
it was better than nothing.

Excited, I went home, sneaking
the bottle in through my window.

In the dead of night, I had my
first drink.
It burned. And I hated it. But
at the same time, I loved the
thrill of it more than the
drinking itself.

But that's not why I drink now.
The thrill is long gone, and
I've gotten much more fucked up
on different things. Now I drink
to make it through the day.

## The Lights Are Off Now

They turned off the lights
today.

I guess that's what happens
When you ignore the bills

Maybe I'll pawn my watch
To turn them back on

But what the hell is the point?

I can write in the dark anyway.

Nothing about me requires the
light.

That realization struck me

I'm still not sure what to think
about it

<u>You</u>

I'd be lying
If I said
I won't be looking
For pieces of you
In every lover
Who comes after
You

## Who Would I Be If I told Myself The Truth

I don't know how I'll feel if this book gets popular. On the one hand, at least someone will hear me and understand my words.

On the other hand, I'll finally have to be honest with myself, with this proof I've written down, uncensored, about who I am.

I can't keep lying to myself, one way or the other. And that's the tragedy of it all.

Who will I be if I tell myself the truth?

## The Curse of Intelligence

The curse of intelligence
Is that it's hard to be happy

I was always sharper
Than anyone else
Smart enough, even, to hide it.

The only way
For people like me
To escape the harsh truths
We can't stop seeing
About life and love

Is to dive in
To a bottle
To breathe poison in
Through a cigarette

We are seeking the bliss
Everyone else has
That beautiful, beautiful bliss
Of ignorance.

## The Greatest Comfort of Sleep

The greatest comfort
Of sleep
Is knowing
Your life, at least,
Will not get worse
while you are asleep.

## X-X105

Don't compare yourself
To others

That is the path
Of conformity

Only compare yourself
To your past self

The only way to win
Is to win against
Yourself

## Wasted Pages

I have thrown away
So many drafts
So many wasted pages
Screaming
My own mediocrity
Back in my face

## The Spirit of Oscar Wilde

I think most people
Are fucking dreadful

Nothing a bit of drink
Can't fix

At least if I dull my mind
I can match them
And perhaps find them
Anything more
Than hopelessly dreadful

## Run Away

You can run away
From your problems
From town to town

But what you're really
Trying to escape
Is yourself

And that is why
You will never
Find happiness
In different places

## When Everything Is Nothing

When you've got nothing to lose
Why not throw it all to the
wind?

Why not risk everything
When everything
Is nothing?

## Rock Bottom

I awake from a dream
Of laying in a field
To find myself
Laying in shattered glass
Cuts and blood all over

A half-shattered bottle
In my left hand
And a pen
With spilled ink
All over my right

Perhaps this is rock bottom
Or glass bottom, as it were

I don't know
Maybe this
Is my last chance
To change

x

## CHAPTER SIX:

ANONYMOUS

## Anonymous

I've fucked up my life
So much
I just want a fresh start
I want to throw it all away

I want to run away to a new
country
I want to leave everything
And be
Anonymous

## Kissing In The Dark

I want to find a pretty woman
Bond over a few drinks
Find a dark room
And kiss
As two souls
Who know nothing
In the entire world
Except this moment

## Who's Gonna Miss Me?

Who will miss me
When I run away?

Who will care
When I go missing?

I guess we shall see.

## Guidance of Fate

Where should I go?

Europe sounds interesting.
I already speak a little
Spanish.

Maybe South America?

Or Asia?

I take a dart in my hand
Close my eyes
And throw it at the map
Of the world

Let fate guide me.

## The Worship of Uncertainty

Why try to plan life
And take fate rigidly
In your hands
Dunking its head
Under the water
And drowning it?

Why fight a battle
We cannot win?

So throw away
All your certainties.

Let fate be your god
Taking you
Where it may

<u>a new beginning.</u>

I packed nothing
But a backpack
With a change of clothes
My passport
And my wallet

Feeling, for the first time
In a long time
That I had some semblance
Of control
Over my life
I sighed a sigh of relief
Smiling at the thought
Of a new life

a new beginning.

## The First Day Abroad

    I was jolted awake as the tires hit the tarmac. My head hurt- another hangover. Not the best way to start my new life in the south of Spain.

    As we were slowly let off the plane, I breathed in the humid air and exhaled the last of R.J. Avenira.

## The Second Day Abroad

I woke up in my hotel room next to a plate of continental breakfast and orange juice. I rubbed my temples out of habit, but realized I didn't have a hangover, as I hadn't drunk myself to sleep last night for the first time in a long time. Perhaps the possibility for change was real this time.

## Alicante

I walked down by the beach
Looking for a woman.

It wasn't long
before I met
Lola.

We spent the day talking
-Me, in broken Spanish
-Her, in broken English

## One Thing Led To Another

Before I knew it, we were back in my hotel. She insisted on drinking, and I wasn't one to disagree.

## Fucked In Alicante

I woke up the next morning
Hungover.
I sat up
On the side of the bed
And noticed
She was gone
But not only that
So was my wallet
My passport
And my phone.

## The Aftermath.

Two weeks later
I was sitting in an airplane
returning home.

So it hadn't gone as I expected
And maybe you expected this
story
To end with me finding myself
But I sure as hell didn't
If anything, I ended up worse
Than before.

<u>But</u>

You can run away
From your town
you can run away
From your life

But

You can't run away
From who you are

X

# CHAPTER SEVEN:

# ROTTED WOOD

## Rotted Wood

Some people
Paint the portrait
Of their lives
In vivid color

But they leave out
The darkness
They leave out
The truth

That's not what I want to do

I don't want to look
Like I have everything
Put together
And be secretly wilting
Inside

I don't want to be
Like a tall tree
That is rotted inside

I want to tell
The whole truth
Hiding nothing
Disguising no darkness

<u>w.a.v.e.s.</u>

Pull me out
From beneath the waves
Show me I'm worth
Being saved

## Frozen Breaths

Today I went back
To the place
Where I first met her

I swear it was haunted

I could see the ghosts
Of our past selves
The frozen breaths
Hanging in the air
The hint of romance
Between here and there

I could hear the sound
Of her laugh
And smell the smell
Of autumn in the air

I went back today
To the place we fell in love
And fell in love with the memory
All over again

## From Dusk To Dawn

Every night I die
And every morning
I come back
From the dead

A different man
Every day
A little more twisted
A little different

From dusk
To Dawn

## People Change You

People change you.

As much as I'd like to think
I made myself the way
That I am
I must acknowledge
The contributions
Of everyone
I've ever loved
And hated
Who made me
Who I am
Today

<u>XXX</u>

I made love
To my dreams
But life
Fucked me

## Time

Time
Will take
The youth
From my face

Time
Will demand
Everything
I have

Age is cruel
Every day that slips by
Is a testament to that fact
It is the only enemy
You can't fight.

## x137

We are all
So damn lost
So damn blind
All looking
For meaning
We will never find

## Apathy

Having an opinion
Is not stupid
Don't let anyone
Convince you
That not caring
Is the answer

The world needs people
Who care
Deeply

And who are willing
To go to any lengths
To achieve the change
They believe
Is necessary

## Women's Rights Are Human Rights

A woman's rights
Are human rights
And a man
Who doesn't respect
Women
Isn't a man
At all.

## These Hard Times

I hope
That I will survive
Through these hard times
I have before
But not like this
Not. Like. This.

x

# CHAPTER EIGHT:

# BLOOD ON MY TYPEWRITER

## Mr. Hemingway

I have taken
Ernest Hemingway's
Advice

I sat down
At my typewriter
And I've let
Every scar
Bleed again
And opened my heart
To the surgery
That is artistic expression

So here I am
Bleeding

I hope that someone
Can see beauty
In this madness

## Issues

She always took issue
When I got jealous
But upon thinking about it
A great deal
I realize
I should've told her
To fuck off
Because if I ever loved her
It was because
She deserved it
If I ever resented her
She deserved it
She earned my love
And my jealousy
Through her actions
And as unimportant as that
May sound
It's important to me
To finally say it.

## Hallow Shell

I am so tired
Of being left out
Of being lonely
Of having no one
To really share
My soul with

I feel as if
Everyone else
Gets to have
A normal life
And I
Am reduced
To settling
For this hallow shell
Of an existence.

I want to live
I want to breathe
I want
To be
Free.

## The Same Shade of Sorrow

Unrequited love
Is the universal
Experience

We have all loved
And not been loved
In return
(at least, not equally)

And that is why
It is so damn powerful
As a subject

We have all
Felt
The same thing
And I think
There's something beautiful
About the fact
That what fundamentally unites
Our species
Is the same shade
Of sorrow.

## Nostalgia For a Virgin Soul

I have become so accustomed
To the pain
That to not feel it
Seems foreign

I can't even remember
What it was like
To feel without fear
Of being hurt
To love without knowing
It will end

What was it like
To be young and free?

Perhaps I will feel it again
In some other life.

## Almost Hemingway

I must confess that earlier today, I took a shotgun and placed the double barrels against the back of my throat. I was hoping that by doing so, I would rekindle some hope of living- perhaps some will to live on would spill over, some primitive instinct to survive would come through and override what I was doing.

The scary thing is, that never happened. There was no voice in my head demanding life- only the calm acceptance of death. That's what scares me. That fear gave me enough will to put the shotgun away and empty it of ammunition, but I remain terrified of what I learned about myself in that moment.

Perhaps Mr. Hemingway has been too much an inspiration.

## I'm a Cancer Anyway

I almost wish
That I were diagnosed
With some terrible,
Incurable illness.

Then, I would feel
Some kind of purpose
To my life

Some kind of divine existence
To guide me
Away from this path
Of brokenness

## Kindred Soul

Is there any kindred soul
In this whole damn universe
Who can understand me?

I feel as though
I am shouting into a void
With every word

No one cares
No one listens
It's all darkness
And I am left here,
Broken.

## Lies

The god
They preach
In church
Is a device
To make money
They're using religion
To get your money
Run away
Run away
From the lies

Content

I got drunk last week
And wandered into the forest
I woke up
Hungover
Looking up at a blue sky
Which peered down at me
Through the tips
Of the trees

It was beautiful
And as birds
Flew across
The canvass
I sighed, content
I wouldn't change
A thing

## If Nothing Else

If nothing else
Be honest
Own what you are
Stand up for your identity

Stop apologizing
For who you are
You don't owe
Anyone
An explanation
For the way
You are

Be true to yourself
If nothing else
Be
Yourself

## The Romantic Parcel Service

I think we've lost something
With the advent
Of texting

We used to have to care
And put work
Into thoughtful messages
Sending them
In elegant envelopes
And waiting for a reply

Excitement ages like wine
Improving with time

But that's no longer the case.

The worst parts of ourselves
Traverse the air instantly
And convenience
Has taken the throne
Of beauty

I'm not advocating a return
To the stone age
But just send a letter
Now and then
To those you care about
Because good things
Take time.

## The Excess of Jaded Souls

It's so easy
To become jaded
In today's modern world
But it's more important
Than ever
To fight that urge

The world needs
People who care
Now more than ever

There are so many battles
That still need to be fought
And apathy
Is the path
Toward's the end
Of us.

## They Deserve The World

The true measure
Of a person's kindness
Is how they treat
People who serve them

It's the small things
That tell all:

How they treat
Fast food workers
Supermarket employees
And service workers

A person
Who is only kind
To their peers
Isn't truly kind;
Their motives
Are selfish

Look for the pure souls
Who never run out
Of kindness
For everyone

They deserve
The world

## Be Patient With Yourself

Life changes
Do not come
All at once

They have to be earned
With a thousand small choices
Over time

Do not expect
To build a city
Overnight

Give yourself some time
Be kind to yourself
When you fail

You will make
The change

Just be patient
With yourself

## True Love Lifts You

If your love
Comes with strings
I don't want
Anything
To do with it

True love
Doesn't come with strings
It comes with wings

## Sobriety

For the first time
In so long
I went a whole week
Without a drink

The days seem so much longer
Than they used to
I don't know
How long
This sobriety will last

If I'm being honest with myself
I doubt I can make it much
longer

But for a person like me
This is a victory
And I've to to take
What I can get

## Pain Into Gold

I never had much money.

I watched as some people
Bought success
Money breeds more money
But I had nothing
And I still have nothing

Perhaps
I can turn my pain
Into gold

Perhaps people
Will sympathize
With my life
And lift me up

Perhaps this pain
Will turn to gold

## The Poet's Heart

The poet's heart
Is full of pain
And beauty

Be kind
For with these words
We bleed
Out innermost pain
Onto the paper
Turning red blood
Into black ink
Hoping the colors
Still translate

## Penultimate

We never become free
Of our demons
We never conquer
The worst parts
Of ourselves

All we can do
Is push them down
And try our best
To let our best selves
Speak

## Blood On My Typewriter

I sat down
At my typewriter
I slit my wrists
And the blood poured out
With every click
Of those blood-sticky keys
I grew closer and closer
To the truth

I needed to bleed out
Everything I was
So that I could become
Everything I need to be

Only by leaving
Everything I am
On these pages
Could I throw
This person away
And become a better man

This is my call to freedom
This is my funeral bell
I'm throwing my soul
In a mass grave

This is the moment
Of my death.